Happy Holidays!

Groundhog Day

by Betsy Rathburn

BELLWETHER MEDIA
MINNEAPOLIS, MN

Blastoff! Beginners are developed by literacy experts and educators to meet the needs of early readers. These engaging informational texts support young children as they begin reading about their world. Through simple language and high frequency words paired with crisp, colorful photos, Blastoff! Beginners launch young readers into the universe of independent reading.

Sight Words in This Book 🔍

a	find	it	out	use
an	have	long	people	we
be	he	make	the	what
come	here	may	they	will
day	in	no	this	
do	is	on	too	

This edition first published in 2024 by Bellwether Media, Inc.

No part of this publication may be reproduced in whole or in part without written permission of the publisher. For information regarding permission, write to Bellwether Media, Inc., Attention: Permissions Department, 6012 Blue Circle Drive, Minnetonka, MN 55343.

Library of Congress Cataloging-in-Publication Data

Names: Rathburn, Betsy, author.
Title: Groundhog Day / by Betsy Rathburn.
Description: Minneapolis, MN : Bellwether Media, Inc., [2024] | Series: Blastoff! Beginners: Happy Holidays! | Includes bibliographical references and index. | Audience: Ages 4-7 years | Audience: Grades K-1
Identifiers: LCCN 2023001661 (print) | LCCN 2023001662 (ebook) | ISBN 9798886873993 (Library Binding) | ISBN 9798886875294 (Paperback) | ISBN 9798886875874 (eBook)
Subjects: LCSH: Groundhog Day--Juvenile literature.
Classification: LCC GT4995.G76 R38 2024 (print) | LCC GT4995.G76 (ebook) | DDC 394.261--dc23/eng/20230120
LC record available at https://lccn.loc.gov/2023001661
LC ebook record available at https://lccn.loc.gov/2023001662

Text copyright © 2024 by Bellwether Media, Inc. BLASTOFF! BEGINNERS and associated logos are trademarks and/or registered trademarks of Bellwether Media, Inc.

Editor: Christina Leaf   Designer: Laura Sowers

Printed in the United States of America, North Mankato, MN.

Table of Contents

It Is Groundhog Day!	4
A Fun Holiday	6
Winter or Spring?	10
Groundhog Day Facts	22
Glossary	23
To Learn More	24
Index	24

It Is Groundhog Day!

Will spring come early? We find out on Groundhog Day!

A Fun Holiday

Groundhog Day is a fun holiday. It is on February 2.

Americans honor it. Canadians do, too.

Groundhog Day in Canada

Winter or Spring?

People guess what the weather will be. They use groundhogs.

Phil is a **famous** groundhog. He is in Pennsylvania.

Phil

Towns may have a party. People wear **costumes**. They dance.

People watch the groundhog. Here it comes!

It may make
a **shadow**.
This means
a longer winter.

It may make no shadow. This means an early spring!

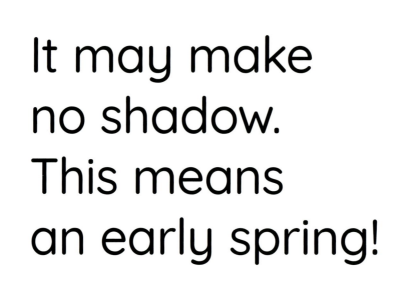

Groundhog Day Facts

Celebrating Groundhog Day

groundhog

shadow

Groundhog Day Activities

watch a groundhog

wear a costume

dance

Glossary

costumes

clothes worn to look like something or someone else

famous

known by many people

shadow

a dark area made by something when light hits it

To Learn More

ON THE WEB

FACTSURFER

Factsurfer.com gives you a safe, fun way to find more information.

1. Go to www.factsurfer.com.

2. Enter "Groundhog Day" into the search box and click 🔍.

3. Select your book cover to see a list of related content.

Index

Americans, 8
Canadians, 8
costumes, 14
dance, 14
February, 6
groundhogs, 10, 12, 16
guess, 10
party, 14
Pennsylvania, 12
Phil, 12, 13
shadow, 18, 20
spring, 4, 20
towns, 14
weather, 10
winter, 18

The images in this book are reproduced through the courtesy of: samray, front cover; Amy Lutz, p. 3; Chris Hondros/ Getty Images, pp. 4-5; Anadolu Agency/ Getty Images, pp. 6-7; Andrew Vaughan/ AP Images, pp. 8, 18; Gene J. Puskar/ AP Images, pp. 8-9; Rabbitt, p. 10; Barry Reeger/ AP Images, pp. 10-11, 12-13; Reuters/ Alamy, pp. 14-15, 22 (wear a costume); Boston Globe/ Getty Images, pp. 16-17, 18-19, 20-21; UlkaStudio, p. 20; Tim Boyle/ Getty Images, p. 22; Adrian Wyle/ AP Images, p. 22 (watch a groundhog); Jeff Swensen, pp. 22 (dance), 23 (costumes, famous); altanaka, p. 23 (shadow).